PEANUTS®

The ICE-SKATING Competition

Based on the comic strips by Charles M. Schulz

Popcorn
ELT
Readers

Peppermint Patty

Peppermint Patty loves sport. She plays baseball in the summer and in the winter she likes to ice-skate. She talks a lot but she doesn't like listening.

Marcie

Marcie and Peppermint Patty are friends. Marcie says 'Sir' to Patty. You say 'Sir' to a teacher, not a friend!

Snoopy

Snoopy is Charlie Brown's
dog. He is very clever.

Charlie Brown

Charlie Brown likes
helping his friends.

Before you read ...
Peppermint Patty is going to an ice-skating
competition. Who can help her learn to ice-skate?

New Words

What do these new words mean? Ask your teacher or use your dictionary.

grumpy

He is **grumpy**.

competition

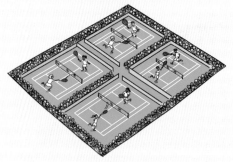

There are a lot of people in the **competition**.

haircut / hairdresser

He is at the **hairdresser**'s. He is having a **haircut**.

dress

Do you like my new **dress**?

ice-skate / ice skates

She can **ice-skate**. She is wearing **ice skates**.

lesson

This is a swimming **lesson**.

roller-skating

They are **roller-skating**.

sew

She is **sewing** some trousers.

sport

What **sport** do you want to play?

wig

He has a lot of **wigs**.

'I've got an idea!'

I've got an idea!

Verbs

Present	Past
fall	fell
feel	felt

PEANUTS

The ICE-SKATING Competition

CHAPTER 1
'I need a teacher'

It was winter and Peppermint Patty was ice-skating.

'You're very good at ice-skating, Sir,' said her friend, Marcie.

'Thanks, Marcie,' said Patty. 'I love ice-skating. And I love baseball. And football. I LOVE ALL SPORTS!' And then ... CRASH! She fell down.

'But I need a teacher,' she said. 'There's a big skating competition soon.'

Peppermint Patty phoned Charlie Brown.
   'There's a skating competition and I want
Snoopy to be my teacher,' she said.
   'Snoopy?' said Charlie. 'Can he ice-skate?'
   'Oh, yes,' said Patty. 'He's very good.'

The next day Peppermint Patty and Snoopy went to the ice.

'What do you think, Snoopy?' Patty asked.

'Bleah!' said Snoopy.

'What about this?'

'Bleah!' said Snoopy.

The lesson was ten dollars. 'That's a lot of money for a lesson,' thought Patty. 'But I need a teacher!'

Marcie watched Peppermint Patty.

'Do you want to ice-skate, Marcie?' asked Peppermint Patty.

'I can't ice-skate, Sir,' said Marcie.

'Snoopy can help you,' said Patty. 'He's grumpy but he's a great teacher.'

'No, thanks,' said Marcie.

CHAPTER 2
'I can't sew, Sir'

Peppermint Patty needed a skating dress for the competition.

'Can you sew, Marcie?' asked Patty. 'Can you make me a dress?'

'No, I can't sew, Sir,' said Marcie.

But Peppermint Patty liked to talk, not listen!
'Great!' she said. 'Let's go to the shops now.'
'Oh no,' thought Marcie. 'But I can't sew!'

Marcie and Peppermint Patty went to the
shops.
'This is exciting,' Patty said.
'I'm not excited,' said Marcie.

The next day Marcie went to see Peppermint Patty.

'Where's the dress, Marcie?' asked Patty.

'Here it is,' said Marcie. 'Do you like it?'

Peppermint Patty was very excited. But then she put on the dress and she didn't like it.

'What is this?' she shouted. 'I can't skate in this dress.'

Peppermint Patty showed the dress to Snoopy.
'Look at this dress,' she cried. 'It's terrible!'
But Snoopy didn't say anything.
   'You are not a very good teacher!' said Patty.
'I'm going to find Charlie Brown.'

Peppermint Patty went to Charlie Brown's house.

'Why are you crying?' he asked.

'This dress is terrible!' she said.

Then Marcie phoned Charlie Brown. 'Hello,' she said. 'Can I talk to you? I feel…' And then she started to cry too.

'Oh no,' said Charlie Brown.

The next day Marcie went to Peppermint Patty's house.

'What do you want?' asked Patty. She was grumpy.

But Marcie smiled. 'I have something for you,' she said.

Marcie showed her a new skating dress.

'My mother made it for you,' said Marcie.

Peppermint Patty was very happy. 'Marcie, Marcie, Marcie, Marcie!' she said. 'This dress is perfect!'

CHAPTER 3
A new haircut

Peppermint Patty went skating in her new dress. She felt great!

But there was still something she had to do.

'I need to change my hair,' said Peppermint Patty.

'Your hair?' asked Marcie. 'Why?'

'It's boring!' she said. 'Please help me!'

'Oh no!' said Marcie. She didn't know much about hair.

Marcie tried to change Peppermint Patty's hair.

'What do you think, Sir?' asked Marcie.

'It's the same!' said Patty. 'Let's do something different.'

Marcie tied up Peppermint Patty's hair.

'How about this?' asked Marcie.

'Something different?' said Peppermint Patty.

But nothing was right.

'I've got an idea!' said Patty.

She went to her friend Charlie Brown.

'I need your help,' she said.

'What's the problem?' asked Charlie Brown.

'I need a haircut for the ice-skating competition. Your dad is a hairdresser. Can he cut my hair?'

'I can ask him,' said Charlie Brown.

Peppermint Patty was at the hairdresser's. She was very excited.

'Hello, Mr Brown,' said Patty. 'I'm Charlie's friend and I'm going to a skating competition. Can you please cut my hair?'

But there was one problem ...

'Look at my hair!' shouted Peppermint Patty.
Her hair was very short. 'Your dad gave me
a boy's haircut! Now I can't go to the skating
competition.'
  'Oh no,' thought Charlie Brown.
  'Bleah,' thought Snoopy.

CHAPTER 4
The competition

Peppermint Patty had an idea. 'I'm going to buy a wig,' she thought. 'I AM going to have beautiful hair.'

She phoned Marcie. 'That's a great idea!' said Marcie. 'Can I see it?'

'OK, but don't laugh,' said Patty.
'OK,' said Marcie.

'Really. Don't laugh.'

'OK, I'm not going to laugh.'

It was the day of the skating competition. Marcie wanted to laugh but she didn't. 'The wig is great!' she said.

Peppermint Patty got on the bus to go to the competition. 'Goodbye!' she said.

There were a lot of people at the competition. Peppermint Patty put on her skates.

The boy next to her looked at her skates. 'You need different skates for this competition,' he said.

'What?' said Patty. Then she saw the boy's skates. 'Oh no!' she said. 'It's a roller-skating competition, not ice-skating!'

Peppermint Patty went back home. She was very sad.

'How was the ice-skating competition?' asked Marcie.

'It wasn't an ice-skating competition, it was a roller-skating competition!' said Patty. 'And now I have to give Snoopy money for all the lessons. But I don't have any money.'

Then she thought of something. 'I know!' she said. 'Snoopy can have my wig!'

Snoopy put on the wig. 'Now *I* need a haircut,' he thought.

THE END

ICE-SKATING COMPETITIONS

Charlie Brown and his friends love ice-skating! They like to skate outside. Peppermint Patty likes skating competitions. Read about some different ice-skating competitions.

Figure skating

Peppermint Patty does figure skating. In this competition skaters jump and spin. They skate to music. Sometimes they throw their partner very high! This skater can spin on one leg!

Did you know?
These are all Winter Olympic sports. The Winter Olympics are every four years.

Speed skating

In speed skating the ice-skaters skate very fast. Some skaters can go 54 kilometres an hour! These men are skating in the Winter Olympics.

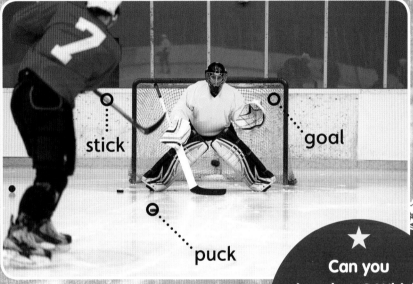

stick

goal

puck

Ice hockey

Ice hockey is a game with two teams. They have to get the puck into the goal with their sticks. The game is dangerous so players wear special clothes.

★
Can you ice-skate? Which ice-skating competition would you like to watch?
★

What do these words mean? Find out.

spin   music   Winter Olympics   team   clothes

After you read

1 True (✓) or false (✗)? Write in the box.

a) Peppermint Patty loves all sports. ✓

b) Marcie wants to ice-skate. ☐

c) Snoopy is a grumpy teacher. ☐

d) Marcie is good at sewing. ☐

e) Patty loves the dress from Marcie's mother. ☐

f) Charlie Brown phones Marcie. ☐

2 Match the sentences with the pictures.

1   2   3   4

a) She wants a new haircut. 1

b) She tries to change Peppermint Patty's hair. ☐

c) His dad is a hairdresser. ☐

d) She thinks Peppermint Patty's wig looks funny. ☐

e) She goes to a roller-skating competition. ☐

f) He puts on the wig. ☐

Where's the popcorn?
Look in your book.
Can you find it?

28

Puzzle time!

1 Do the puzzle and answer the question.

When can you go ice-skating outside?

In ....

2 Circle five more past tense verbs from the story in the ice skate below. Then find the words in your book.

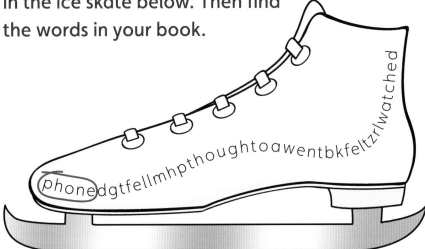

3 What sport is Snoopy doing? Complete
the picture.

4a What other sports do you know? Write a list
of four.

....

....

....

....

b Work in pairs. Mime a sport. Your friend guesses
the sport.

Imagine...

Your teacher is going to read the story. When the whistle blows, say the missing word.

For example:

It was winter and Peppermint Patty was  .

ice-skating!

'You're very good at ice-skating, Sir,' said her friend, 🎵 .

Marcie!

Chant

1 (T 8) **Listen and read.**

Let's ice-skate!

One, two, three, four!
Are you ready?
Open the door!

Five, six, seven, eight!
Now go outside
And let's ice-skate!

One, two, three, four!   Five, six, seven, eight!
I love skating.   Jump up and spin,
Let's do some more!   Skating is great!

2 (T 9) **Say the chant.**